GREEN HOPEX

The Steadfast Retirement Devotional for Men

52 Weeks of 3-Minute Devotions for Gifts of Faith, Purpose, and Building a Legacy in Your Next Chapter

First edition

This book was professionally typeset on Reedsy.
Find out more at reedsy.com

Contents

Your Beautiful Next Season

Week 1 - New Season, Same Lord

"*So teach us to number our days, that we may apply our hearts unto wisdom.*" *- Psalm 90:12*

The first Monday after I retired felt strange. No alarm. No commute. No inbox waiting for me. I poured coffee and stared at a calendar that had more white space than I had seen in forty years. My heart felt light for a moment, then heavy. I walked the hallway, picking up little chores, but I kept checking the clock like I was late for something that did not exist.

By lunch, I was restless and a bit grumpy. My wife asked, "What do you want this day to be?" I shrugged. That was the problem. My days used to be decided by meetings and deadlines. Now I had a wide field and no idea where to step. I felt useless, and that bothered me more than I wanted to admit.

That afternoon I opened an old Bible that sat on my desk at work for years. The ribbon was in Psalm 90. The words hit hard: "Teach us to number our days." I had counted hours for decades, squeezing every minute to get the job done. Wisdom is different. Wisdom counts a day not by tasks, but by purpose. Retirement changed my calendar, not my calling. God still wanted my heart alive to Him and my hands ready to love people.

I grabbed my phone and set the first appointment on my empty schedule: "God at 7:30 a.m." Fifteen minutes. Bible open. Quiet prayer. A simple song whisper. The next morning, when that reminder chimed, I felt anchored. I was not drifting anymore. I was meeting with the same Lord who guided me on busy days. He could guide me in quiet ones too.

That small block on my calendar did not feel small at all. It felt like the first stake in the ground for a new field.

Prayer

Teach me to number my days with wisdom. Father, calm the noise inside me and set my pace. Meet me in the quiet and show me what matters today. Shape my plans, my rest, and my service. Let every open space become a place You fill with purpose. Amen.

Practical Step

Block a 15-minute daily God appointment on your calendar.

Week 2 - From Title to Identity

"Fear not: for I have redeemed thee, I have called thee by thy name; thou art mine."
- Isaiah 43:1

I handed in my badge and key at HR, and the door clicked behind me. It was a small sound, but it echoed in my chest. For years, that badge opened rooms, brought respect, and told people who I was. Walking to the car, my hands felt empty. At home, I slid the badge into a drawer and shut it. Then I stood there, staring at the wood like I had just buried part of myself.

The next morning, I brewed coffee and opened my Bible. Isaiah 43 was on the reading plan. The words felt personal, almost like God spoke my name out loud: "I have called you by name; you are mine." A wave of relief came first, then a sting. I realized how much weight I had put on my title to prop up my sense of worth. Titles fade. God's naming sticks.

That afternoon my grandson barreled into the house yelling, "Grandpa!" He did not care about what I used to do. He cared that I was his. Later, when a neighbor asked, "So what did you do?" I almost answered with my old line. Instead, I tried something new: "I am a follower of Jesus, a husband, a grandpa. I used to work in operations." It felt humble, but it also felt true.

I wrote three words on a small card: son, disciple, steward. I tucked it in my wallet where my badge used to sit. Every time I reach for my ID, I see who I am before what I do. It changes how I enter a room. I am not chasing a name. I am carrying one God already gave me.

Prayer

Root my identity in You, not in work. Father, strip away labels that do not last. Remind me that I am Your son, called by Your name, held by Your love. Let every conversation and choice flow from who I am in Christ, not what I used to do. Amen.

Practical Step

Write three God-given identities (e.g., son, disciple, steward) on a card; keep it in your wallet.

Week 3 - A Rule of Life

"And whatsoever ye do in word or deed, do all in the name of the Lord Jesus." - Colossians 3:17

The first month of retirement, I tried to do everything. Gym three days, golf twice, read a book a week, volunteer, fix the fence, learn the guitar. By week two, I was tired and behind on all of it. The list was loud. My soul was not. One afternoon I stepped into the garden and stared at our tomato plants. They looked strong, but the vines were starting to flop. I grabbed some twine and tied them to the posts. A simple support changed everything. The plants did not lose freedom. They found direction.

I realized my days needed the same thing. I had been trying to sprint without a path. A rule of life is not a prison. It is a simple set of supports that keep what matters from falling over. The verse from Colossians came to mind. If everything can be done in Jesus' name, then nothing is too small to be holy when it is done with Him and for Him.

I sat at the table and wrote a starter rule. One daily habit: Scripture before phone. One weekly habit: a true Sabbath, even if it starts small. One monthly habit: serve someone outside my circle. I opened my calendar and put them in. No vague hopes. Actual dates and times.

The first week felt different. Scripture before phone quieted the panic that liked to rush in early. A weekly Sabbath gave a finish line and a beginning. That monthly serve day made me look beyond my comfort. My days were not packed, but they were pointed. Freedom with a frame.

Prayer

Align my habits with Your glory. Lord Jesus, set up simple supports that keep my heart steady. Show me what to start, what to stop, and what to schedule. Make ordinary moments holy as I do them with You. Let this rule be flexible, but faithful, and keep me close. Amen.

Practical Step

Choose 1 daily habit (Scripture), 1 weekly (Sabbath), 1 monthly (serve) and schedule them.

Week 4 - Holy Rest Without Drifting

"Come unto me, all ye that labour and are heavy laden, and I will give you rest... my yoke is easy, and my burden is light." - Matthew 11:28–30

At first, I treated rest like a couch. I napped when I wanted, scrolled until my thumb hurt, and told myself I had earned it. A week later, I felt foggy and oddly empty. Rest without purpose turned into drift. Too many open hours started to blur the edges of my days.

One morning I read Jesus' words about rest and His yoke. I pictured two oxen side by side, pulling together. Rest was not escape. It was shared work with a gentle Leader. His pace. His path. His strength. I realized I had taken off all yokes and was wandering fields I did not need to cross.

I made a small plan. Early walk with prayer. Light chores with worship music. One phone call to encourage someone. A simple project after lunch. I kept the tone gentle, not harsh. Resting in Christ did not mean doing nothing. It meant recovering as I moved with Him.

By the end of the day, my body felt better, and my mind was clear. I slept deeper that night. Over the next week, I set fixed times to sleep and wake, and my energy changed. The point was not perfection. It was partnership. Rest is recovery, not retreat from purpose. Jesus' yoke does not crush. It carries.

Prayer

Give me Your rest and Your yoke. Lord, slow my hurry and steady my drift. Teach me to stop without guilt and to move with You without strain. Fill my rest with Your presence so my work and relationships are refreshed. Lead me into a rhythm that heals. Amen.

Practical Step

Establish fixed sleep and wake times for 7 days.

Week 5 - Gratitude That Grounds

"In every thing give thanks: for this is the will of God in Christ Jesus concerning you." - 1 Thessalonians 5:18

The market dipped, the faucet leaked, and the weather canceled our plans. By afternoon, my mood was sinking with the rain. I caught myself muttering, "Nothing goes right." That sentence tasted bitter as soon as I said it. I opened my journal and stared at a blank page, then wrote three lines: hot coffee, text from a friend, the steady way my wife hums when she cooks.

It felt small, almost silly. But as I wrote, my shoulders dropped. Gratitude did not ignore what was wrong. It let me see what was still good. I remembered Paul's words about giving thanks in everything, not for everything. There is always something to name, even on hard days. Thankfulness is not a mood. It is a choice that steadies the heart.

I kept the practice the next morning. Three lines. No pressure to make it deep. Just honest thanks. The list grew over the week. A sunrise through gray clouds. A neighbor's wave. A story from my grandson that made me laugh. The more I noticed, the more there was to notice. Gratitude grounded me in the present when my mind wanted to spin into worry.

By the weekend, I realized something simple. Thankfulness does not shrink pain, but it keeps it from filling the whole frame. It gives me a wider view where God's quiet gifts are still in the picture. Retirement has its unknowns. Gratitude is how I stay steady in them.

Prayer

Open my eyes to today's gifts. Father, train my heart to notice Your kindness in small and simple things. When worry rises, turn my mind toward thanks. Let gratitude shape my words, my tone, and my choices, so I live from joy and not fear. Fill this day with praise. Amen.

Practical Step

Start a 3-line daily gratitude log.

Week 6 - Courage For Change

"Be strong and of a good courage... for the Lord thy God is with thee whithersoever thou goest." - Joshua 1:9

I saw a flyer for a men's group at church and almost walked past it. New faces. New routine. New anything made my stomach tighten. At work, I knew my place. Out here, I felt like the new kid in the lunchroom again. I told myself I would think about it, which usually means no.

That night I read Joshua's charge. Be strong. Be courageous. Not because Joshua was fearless, but because God promised to be with him. Courage is not the absence of fear. It is movement with God in the middle of it. I picked up the flyer and called the number. My voice shook a little while I left a message.

The first meeting, I sat by the door. The guys were kind. They talked about real things. One man shared about a health scare, another about his anger. I spoke up near the end. It felt risky. It also felt like fresh air. The next week, it was easier to walk in. Change did not feel like a cliff. It felt like a small step on solid ground.

Courage for change showed up elsewhere too. I tried a new volunteer role. I watched a tutorial to learn a tool I had avoided. Each time, the fear shrank after the first move. God's presence outmuscled my uncertainty. Not because I got strong on my own, but because I was not alone.

Prayer

Make me strong and courageous in You. Lord, meet me in my fear and help me take the next faithful step. Remind me You go before me and stay with me. Turn new spaces into places where I see Your hand. Let obedience be my courage. Amen.

Practical Step

List one change you fear; take one small action toward it.

Week 7 - Redeeming Mornings

"My voice shalt thou hear in the morning, O Lord; in the morning will I direct my prayer unto thee, and will look up." - Psalm 5:3

For years my mornings were rushed. In retirement they got slow, but not holy. I grabbed my phone, drifted through headlines, and lost half an hour without meaning to. One morning, I set the phone in another room and started a simple ten-minute liturgy. Coffee ready the night before. Bible open to the next reading. A short prayer, then one planned act of service for the day.

The room was quiet. Birds worked the dawn. I read a short Psalm and prayed out loud, just a few honest lines. I wrote one name to encourage and one small job to bless my home. The whole thing took less time than the news, but it left me calm and awake inside.

After a week, mornings felt redeemed. It was not fancy, and I did not always feel spiritual. But starting with God first changed the rest of the day. When small annoyances popped up, I had already looked up. When choices came, I had already set my heart. Winning the morning helped me win the day.

I learned to keep it light, not legalistic. If I missed a day, I returned the next with joy, not guilt. The point was meeting a Person, not checking a box. The morning became a doorway I stopped rushing through and started walking into with God.

Prayer

Meet me first, Lord. Draw my attention to You before the noise begins. Speak through Your Word, steady my thoughts, and set my hands to a simple act of love. Let these first minutes shape every other moment, so I carry Your peace and purpose all day. Amen.

Practical Step

Create a 10-minute morning liturgy: read, pray, plan one service act.

Week 8 - Sabbath As Anchor

"The sabbath was made for man, and not man for the sabbath." - Mark 2:27

Sundays had turned into catch-up days. Laundry, errands, random fixes. I told myself I was free now, but my soul felt thin. Then I remembered Jesus' words. Sabbath is a gift, not a rule to crush me. It is God's oxygen for tired hearts. I asked my wife if we could try a true 24-hour Sabbath. She smiled, like she had been waiting for me to ask.

We picked a time from dinner Saturday to dinner Sunday. We planned worship, a simple meal we could prep early, a walk at our favorite park, and a short list of things that help us delight. We also chose what to refrain from: chores, email, scrolling, and hard conversations.

When the time started, we put our phones in a drawer. The quiet felt wide. We sat longer at dinner and said thanks for specific gifts from the week. Sunday morning we worshiped, then napped. We took that walk, stopping to watch kids race leaves in the creek. It all felt slow and kind.

On Monday, my mind was clearer. Decisions felt easier. The week had a steady start. I realized Sabbath does not steal time. It gives it back, since rest makes the other six days work the way they should. Sabbath is not a luxury. It is oxygen for the soul and an anchor for this new season.

Prayer

Teach me to stop without guilt. Lord of the Sabbath, help me receive Your gift with joy. Guard this time from hurry and from my need to control. Fill it with worship, rest, delight, and love. Let Sabbath restore my body and re-center my heart on You. Amen.

Practical Step

Plan a 24-hour Sabbath this week: worship, rest, delight, refrain.

Week 9 - Time Budget Beats Lists

"Look carefully then how you walk, not as unwise but as wise, making the best use of the time." (Ephesians 5:15–16)

The week after I retired, I made a to-do list so long it looked like a receipt from a warehouse store. Fix the fence. Organize the attic. Take the grandkids fishing. Read the prophets. Start volunteering. I felt proud for ten minutes, then heavy in my chest. By Thursday the list still glared at me, and I felt like I had lost a job but kept the pressure.

That night, I noticed how I used to guard money with care. I made a budget, avoided waste, and gave first. Why did hours get less respect than dollars? Ephesians pressed on me: make the best use of time. If time is a gift, I should plan it like a gift, not cram it like a closet.

I grabbed a blank page and wrote five words across the top: faith, family, service, fitness, fun. Under each, I penciled a number of hours for the week, like a spending plan. Faith: 5 hours. Family: 8. Service: 4. Fitness: 4. Fun: 5. I blocked them on my calendar. The list did not vanish, but it had to line up behind the budget.

The next day I kept a quiet hour with Scripture and prayer before anything else. Saturday morning I shut the garage door at 9:30 because I had "family" on the calendar. We showed up for my grandson's soccer game without rushing, and I watched his eyes search the sideline until he saw us. That smile was worth more than crossing off ten chores.

By Sunday, I felt lighter. The fence still needed paint, but my week had fruit, not just activity. Budgeting time taught me a simple truth: tasks will expand to fill every corner unless purpose sets the walls. Budget hours like dollars, and you will feel rich where it matters.

Prayer

Lord, You are the giver of days. Teach me to number my hours with wisdom. Help me invest first in what You value, not what shouts the loudest. Guard me from busywork that steals joy. Let my calendar reflect love, worship, and steady purpose. In Jesus' name, amen.

Practical Step

Allocate a simple weekly time budget across five buckets: faith, family, service, fitness, and fun. Put the hours on your calendar.

A Moment with God

Which bucket has been underfunded in your life, and what specific hour will you invest in it this week?

Week 10 - Distraction Detox

"Be still, and know that I am God." (Psalm 46:10)

I used to wake up and reach for my phone before my glasses. Headlines, baseball scores, weather radar, group chats, and a quick peek at the market. By the time coffee brewed, my soul already felt like a crowded hallway. Retirement gave me more free time, but noise filled it fast.

One morning my wife asked, "Do you ever hear the birds anymore?" I paused. There was a soft chorus outside, and I had missed it for weeks. Psalm

46:10 came to mind like a gentle command. Be still. Not busy. Not informed. Still.

I decided to try a seven-day experiment. No screens for the first and last thirty minutes of each day. The first morning was awkward. My thumb twitched for a screen. Instead, I sat by the window, breathed slow, and read a Psalm out loud. The quiet felt thin at first, like I was wasting time. Then it felt thick, like honey settling. I could hear the birds. I could hear my own thoughts. I could hear God, not with my ears but with a calmer heart.

Evenings changed too. Instead of scrolling until my eyes ached, I took a slow walk, cleaned the kitchen with music, and had a simple prayer before bed. By day four, my mind felt less jumpy. I noticed neighbors. I remembered names. The market still moved, but my soul did not swing with it.

Chronic noise kills purpose because it crowds out presence. Distraction promises relief, but it steals attention, which is the soil where calling grows. Be still, and you remember who holds the world and your next chapter.

Prayer

Father, quiet the inner storm. Turn down the volume of my feeds and fears so I can hear Your voice. Teach me to enjoy simple silence. Meet me there with peace and direction. Make stillness a daily place, not a rare event. In Jesus' name, amen.

Practical Step

Practice a 7-day phone fast: no screens for the first and last 30 minutes of each day. Use that time for Scripture, prayer, or a quiet walk.

A Moment with God

What noise steals your attention most, and what simple swap will you make in the quiet space you reclaim?

Week 11 - Guard Your Yes

"Above all else, guard your heart, for everything you do flows from it." (Proverbs 4:23)

After I retired, people started calling with good things. Coach the church softball team. Join the board for the food pantry. Help with a fishing clinic. Each request felt like a compliment. I kept saying yes, because serving is right. But after a month, my calendar looked like a patchwork quilt, stitched without a pattern. I was busy, but not peaceful. My wife gently asked, "Do you have anything left for home?"

That night, I saw it clearly. Guard your heart. Not to hoard your life, but to protect your best from a thousand good distractions. Saying yes to everything had become saying no to my health, my marriage, and unhurried time with God. Guarding my yes would let me serve better, not less.

I wrote a simple filter on an index card: Does this align with my mission, my gifts, and my current capacity? If two out of three were no, my answer would be no. The next day a friend asked me to lead a new fundraiser. It was noble, but it did not fit my focus this season. My heart thumped as I replied with a kind no and a promise to pray and give. He thanked me anyway. I hung up and felt relief, not guilt.

A week later, I had the space to sit with a neighbor who just lost his wife. No agenda, just presence. That quiet afternoon mattered more than another meeting ever could. Guarding my yes protected my best.

Prayer

Lord, give me courage to say no when my yes would crowd out what You have entrusted to me. Teach me wise boundaries. Help me serve from a full heart, not a frantic one. Show me where You want me, and give me grace to release the rest. Amen.

Practical Step

Write a polite "no" template and use it once this week.

A Moment with God

Where has a good yes been stealing from your best yes, and what will you protect this week?

Week 12 - One-Line Mission

"He has shown you, O man, what is good; and what does the Lord require of you but to act justly, love mercy, and walk humbly with your God." (Micah 6:8)

Retirement felt like a wide field with no fence posts. I had freedom, but I drifted. One afternoon over coffee, a friend asked, "If you had one line to describe your next chapter, what would it be?" I stared at the table. I could list interests, but no mission.

Micah 6:8 gave me anchors: justice, mercy, humility. I scribbled drafts that were either too long or too vague. Then I tried this: "Walk close with God, love my family well, and build hope where it is thin." It was simple, but it felt like a spine. Decisions suddenly had a ruler.

When a neighbor asked me to mentor boys at the community center, it fit "build hope where it is thin." When I was tempted to take another committee seat, it did not fit. The mission was not a cage. It was a compass. I taped the sentence where I plan my week and read it out loud each morning. It trimmed wasted motion and brought quiet confidence. A clear mission does that. It saves you from trying to do everything and frees you to do the right things with love.

Prayer

Father, clarify my assignment in this season. Give me words that aim my days toward Your heart. Keep my mission rooted in Your Word, not my pride. Help me walk humbly, love mercy, and do what blesses others. Make my one line a lived line. In Jesus' name, amen.

Practical Step

Draft a 20-word life mission and post it where you plan your week.

A Moment with God

Write your one-line mission now. How will it change one decision you are facing this week?

Week 13 - Projects Not Piles

"They said, 'Let us rise up and build.' So they strengthened their hands for the good work." (Nehemiah 2:18)

Our garage had become a museum of good intentions. Boxes labeled "photos," "tools," and "misc" sat like silent judges. Every time I went out there, I felt a mix of guilt and confusion. Where do you even start with a mountain of piles?

Nehemiah stirred me. He did not move rubble around. He named the work, rallied help, and set checkpoints. I pulled a fresh notebook and wrote, "Family History Wall project." Not boxes. A project. Then I set a 30-day window with weekly checkpoints: Week 1, sort. Week 2, select and scan. Week 3, design layout. Week 4, mount and celebrate.

I told my family and scheduled Saturday mornings. The first week, we laughed over old photos and tossed blurry duplicates. The second week, I learned basic scanning and asked my tech-savvy grandson for help. He felt proud to teach me. By week three, the idea moved from fog to shape. On day thirty, we stood in the hallway and looked at four generations smiling back at us. The garage still had boxes, but we had finished a project that brought joy and story into our home.

Named projects get finished because they have edges, energy, and an end. Piles demand nothing and give nothing. Call it what it is, set a timeline, and ask for help. You will feel momentum instead of dread.

Prayer

Lord, prosper the work of my hands. Give me courage to name the next project and wisdom to plan simple steps. Bring the right people alongside me. Help me finish what I start, not for pride, but for blessing. Let the work build more than walls. In Jesus' name, amen.

Practical Step

Choose one 30-day project and set weekly checkpoints to track progress.

A Moment with God

What pile will you rename as a project today, and what is your first small step this week?

Week 14 - The Daily Three

"Commit to the Lord whatever you do, and He will establish your plans." (Proverbs 16:3)

I used to wake up and try to tackle fifteen things. By lunch I had started many and finished none. The day felt like a scattershot. My energy was spent in the shuffle. One morning I tried something different. Before coffee, I prayed Proverbs 16:3 and wrote three priorities for the day. Not twelve. Three.

I chose what mattered most to God and the people I love. Call my brother and reconcile. Walk two miles. Finish the letter to my grandson. I put those three at the top of a sticky note and promised to do them before lunch.

The focus felt strange at first, like I was ignoring worthy tasks. But by noon I had peace in my bones. The call led to laughter and a plan to visit. The walk cleared my mind. The letter became a keepsake. The rest of the list? It waited, and that was fine. Three priorities beat fifteen wishes because attention is finite and wins are contagious. Stack small wins, and your days gain a rhythm of purpose.

Prayer

Lord, establish what matters today. Help me choose the right three and give me strength to finish them with love. Keep me from being pulled in every direction. Let my priorities reflect Your heart and bring peace to my home. I commit my work to You. Amen.

Practical Step

Each morning, write your top three and do them before lunch.

A Moment with God

If you could only finish three things today that honor God and people, what are they?

Week 15 - Sacred Margin

"Jesus said, 'Who touched me?' ... Then He said to her, 'Daughter, your faith has made you well; go in peace.'" (Luke 8:43–48)

I once packed my day edge to edge. Every appointment touched the next. I felt efficient, until real life knocked. One Tuesday, on my way to a doctor's visit, a neighbor waved me down. His car would not start, and he needed to get to his wife's appointment across town. I looked at my watch and felt the tug. If I helped, I would be late. If I kept driving, I would be on time but miss a chance to love.

I remembered Jesus on His way to heal a girl. He stopped for a woman in pain who reached for Him in a crowd. That interruption became the miracle. I pulled over and said, "Hop in." We made it in time. My clinic rescheduled me without drama. On the drive back, my neighbor opened up about fear and faith. We prayed in the parking lot. God often travels in interruptions.

Since then, I leave fifteen-minute buffers between appointments. That margin turned strangers into conversations and small needs into ministry. I have helped pick up a dropped bag of groceries, listened to a worried young dad, and said a proper goodbye to a friend in the church hallway instead of rushing past. Margin protects compassion.

Prayer

Jesus, make me interruptible. I want to walk at Your pace, not hurry past people You love. Give me courage to leave space and wisdom to see moments You send. Use my buffers to bring peace and hope to others. Let interruptions become stories of Your care. Amen.

Practical Step

Leave 15-minute buffers between appointments all week. Use the space to notice and serve.

A Moment with God

Where can you create a small buffer today, and who might God place in that space for you to love?

Week 16 - Bless Your Spouse

"Each husband must love his wife as himself, and the wife must respect her husband."
(Ephesians 5:33)

Insight: Appreciation breaks criticism cycles.

I did not notice how sharp I sounded until I heard my wife fall silent. It was a small thing. She set a new picture on the mantel, and I said, "It is a little crooked." The room cooled. I told myself I was being helpful, but the truth was simpler. I had gotten lazy about gratitude.

Later, I stood at the sink, hands in warm water, replaying the day. I could list ten things she did that made our home gentle and steady. I had not voiced even one. Ephesians 5 came to mind, not as a rule, but as a mirror. Love and respect are not theories. They show up in tones, glances, and words. If love is a coat, I had been handing her thin fabric.

The next morning I tried something different. Before she woke up, I wrote a small note and left it by her coffee mug: "Thank you for how you make this house a haven. I see you. I choose you." When she found it, her eyes filled. No speech. Just a soft smile that said, "I feel safe."

That day, each time my mind reached for a critique, I paused and named something good: the way she remembers birthdays, the patience she shows our grandkids, the faith that steadies me when I wobble. I watched her shoulders relax. Mine did too. Appreciation did not erase hard conversations, but it broke the cycle that made small issues feel big.

Love and respect are daily seeds. Criticism can feel quick and smart, but it makes poor soil. Blessing takes aim at what is lovely and waters it. The vineyard grows again when we notice buds and cheer them on. My realization was simple and strong. I can choose the words that build.

Prayer

Lord Jesus, soften my tone; sharpen my gratitude. Train my mouth to bless, not to nitpick. Show me fresh ways to honor my wife in word, touch, and service. Heal patterns of criticism I have learned. Fill our home with patient love that mirrors Yours. Amen. Today and every day.

A Moment with God

What is one specific quality in your spouse you can praise out loud today?

Practical Step

Speak one specific affirmation today.

Week 17 - Listening that Heals

"Be quick to listen, slow to speak, slow to anger." (James 1:19)

Insight: Slow ears save relationships.

My son called on a Tuesday night. I could hear tightness in his voice, the kind that wraps around a sentence and squeezes. He started, "Dad, work has been rough." I jumped in fast. "You should talk to your boss. Have you tried a planner? Here is what I would do." The line went quiet, then thin. He said, "Thanks," and changed the subject. After we hung up, the room felt heavy.

James wrote about slow speech for a reason. My quick answers did not heal. They made him feel unknown. The next day, I called back and said, "Son, yesterday I talked too much. Can I listen?" He exhaled. I tried the three questions I had written on a sticky note: "Tell me more. What matters most right now? How can I help?" That little trio opened a door.

He talked about feeling overlooked at meetings, about a project he loved, about doubt. I did not fix. I nodded, asked, "Anything else?" and waited. The anger that had started to rise in me the night before faded. I felt curious instead of controlling. He ended with, "Thanks, Dad. I needed that." So did I.

Listening is slow work. It feels like doing nothing, yet it is the work that makes room for God to move. When I hold back my opinions, I leave space for trust to grow. My son did not need a coach in that moment. He needed a father who would hear his heart. Quick ears saved the call, and maybe seeds of future calls too.

Prayer

Father, teach me to listen first. Put a guard over my lips. Make me quick with patience, slow with opinions, and slower with anger. Help me ask wise questions and hear the heart beneath the words. Use my quiet to heal those I love. Amen. Shape me into a listener.

A Moment with God

Whose story needs your full attention this week, and what three questions will you ask?

Practical Step

Use the 3-question rule before advice: "Tell me more… What matters most? How can I help?"

Week 18 - Dating Your Wife (Again)

"Arise, my love, come away… For winter is past, flowers appear on the earth." (Song of Songs 2:10–13)

Insight: Pursuit keeps warmth alive.

Retirement gave me time, but somehow our marriage felt cooler, like a room with a vent partly closed. We had traded adventure for errands. One Friday I told my wife, "Let us do something fun," and then I stared at the budget and sighed. I believed romance needed reservations and money. Song of Songs nudged me. The Lover invites with simple beauty. No tickets required.

I grabbed a blanket, two mugs, and the cheap cocoa we keep for grandkids. I set a sunset picnic in our backyard, under the maple that has held our seasons. I printed a small set of prompts: "What did you notice about me when we first met? What makes you feel chosen now? What would feel fun this month?" When she stepped outside, the sky glowed pink. So did her cheeks.

We talked and laughed until the solar lights blinked on. I told her I still see the girl who beat me at putt-putt, the woman who prays me steady. She told me she misses our old habit of slow walks. We planned a weekly low-cost date, and we wrote it on the calendar like it mattered, because it does.

Pursuit is not about grand gestures. It is about attention with feet. The warmth returned because I moved first, again, and again. Winter passed in our yard long before spring came to town. My breakthrough was simple. Romance grows where I plant it, protect it, and enjoy it, even if dinner is peanut butter sandwiches and a shared blanket.

Prayer

Lord, renew our delight. Wake up playful wonder in our marriage. Give me creativity to pursue my wife with kindness, laughter, and time. Sweep away boredom, grudges, and screens. Help me notice her beauty again and say so. Let our love reflect Your faithful joy. Amen. Tonight, tomorrow, and beyond.

A Moment with God

What low-cost date would make your wife feel chosen this week?

Practical Step

Schedule a weekly low-cost date and protect it.

Week 19 - Adult Children & Honor

"If possible, as far as it depends on you, live at peace with everyone." (Romans 12:18)

Insight: Influence requires respect, not control.

At our daughter's house, I saw toys on the floor, dishes stacked, and a bedtime that kept slipping. The coach in me woke up. I began lining up tips in my head. Then I watched my daughter kneel by a tired toddler and whisper a silly song that turned tears into giggles. I felt the Spirit tap my shoulder. She is not my project. She is my child.

Romans 12:18 pulled me toward peace. As far as it depends on me, not as far as it depends on them agreeing with me. I pictured all the moments I had given advice without an invitation. Even helpful words can feel heavy. Respect is lighter. It says, "I see you. I trust God's work in you."

That night, instead of entering the kitchen with suggestions, I asked, "How can I help?" She handed me a dish towel and said, "Thanks, Dad." We talked about books and her new hopes for work. She opened up about a worry. She asked for prayer, not a plan. I prayed like a fellow pilgrim.

Influence grew right there, not because I controlled the scene, but because I honored her space. Peace came when I let go of the need to be right and held tight to the call to be loving. The next morning I sent a simple text: "Proud of you. I believe in you. Here if you want help." She replied with a heart. Respect builds bridges where control builds walls.

Prayer

God, grant me humility and patience. Teach me to show respect to my adult children, not control. Help me weigh words, wait my turn, and withdraw advice when unasked. Make me a calm, steady presence who blesses and believes the best. Use me to build peace. Amen. Today, tomorrow, always.

A Moment with God

Where have you been offering unasked advice, and what respectful words could you send instead?

Practical Step

Send a no-advice encouragement text to each child.

Week 20 - Grandfather on Purpose

"We will tell the next generation the praiseworthy deeds of the Lord." (Psalm 78:4)

Insight: Grandfathers are memory-makers of God's works.

My grandson asked why my hands are speckled. I told him they are maps, showing where I have been. He climbed into my lap and said, "Tell me a story." In the past, I would have waved him off with a joke. Not this time. Psalm 78 stirred me. My stories are gifts, not old news.

I built a little tradition that day. I pulled out my phone, opened the voice recorder, and titled a note, "Grandpa Stories." I told him about the night his dad was born, how scared I was when the nurse whisked him away, and how God met me in a quiet hallway with a strange peace. I kept it simple. He listened with wide eyes. Later, I texted the audio to our family thread. Replies dinged like applause in a small theater.

The next week I recorded another one. I talked about losing my job years ago, how we almost lost the house, how a neighbor showed up with groceries and cash in an envelope, and how that taught me to trust God's timing. My granddaughter drew a picture of a bag of apples and taped it to our fridge.

I realized I do not need to be a perfect teacher. I need to be a faithful witness. Grandfathering on purpose looks like schedules and stories, like letting a child stir pancake batter while I tell about prayer in a hospital parking lot. Memories become altars when we mark them and share them. I want my grandkids to know their family's God is alive.

Prayer

Father, help me tell the next generation. Put Your works on my tongue and in my schedule. Give me stories, patience, and energy to play, teach, and pray. Let my grandchildren hear hope from my mouth and see grace in my actions. Make me faithful and fun. Amen. All year.

A Moment with God

Which story of God's faithfulness will you record for your family this week?

Practical Step

Start a monthly "Grandpa Story" (audio note) about God's faithfulness.

Week 21 - Friendship beyond the Locker Room

"Iron sharpens iron, and one man sharpens another." (Proverbs 27:17)
Insight: Real friends sharpen, not flatter.

After I retired, my conversations got thin. We talked sports, aches, and weather. Nothing sharp. I missed the challenge of a teammate who would tell me when I had spinach in my soul. One Sunday, a man named Luis shook my hand and said, "Coffee this week?" I almost dodged. I am glad I did not.

We met at a small shop that smells like hope and roasted beans. We traded stories about work, regrets, and what God is doing now. I decided to risk honesty. I said, "I have been numb lately. Lazy with prayer. Quick to judge." He did not flinch. He asked, "What do you want God to change first?" Then he told me his struggle with anger and how he is learning to pause.

We left with a simple plan. Every other Thursday, same table. Two honest questions each. One thing to obey before we meet again. No pretending. The first week, he asked me if I had told my wife the appreciation I felt. I had not. I did that night. The next time, I asked him if he had apologized to his son. He had, and it went better than he feared.

Sharpening is not about winning an argument. It is about losing dullness. Real friends do not just nod. They knock on the door of your heart with courage and care. My life feels lighter and stronger because a brother sits across from me with truth and grace. We both leave with edges that can bless.

Prayer

Lord, give me iron-sharpens-iron companions. Lead me to men who love You and tell the truth. Make me brave to be honest, humble to be corrected, and loyal to encourage. Use our conversations to shape character, courage, and joy for Your glory. Keep us steady. Amen. Today and every week.

A Moment with God

Who is one man you will invite for sharpening friendship, and what two honest questions will you bring?

Practical Step

Invite one man for coffee with two honest questions each.

Week 22 - Reconciling Old Wounds

"If you remember someone has something against you, go and be reconciled." (Matthew 5:23–24)

Insight: Reconciliation is kingdom work.

There is a man named Carl I avoided for ten years. We had a business deal go sideways. Words got sharp. Pride took root. Every time I saw his name on social media, my stomach tightened. I told myself time would heal it. Time only taught me how to dodge.

Matthew 5 called me out. Worship is not a cover for a broken relationship. God cares about the courage to make peace. I wrote Carl a short message: "I am sorry for my part. I blamed you to protect my ego. If you are willing, I would like to make this right." I hit send and felt my hands tremble.

He replied the next day. "Thank you. I was wrong too. Coffee?" We met in a place with brick walls and second chances. I named the ways I had failed, specifically. No excuses. He did the same. The air felt cleaner with each sentence. We did not become best friends in one hour, but we ended a war. We agreed to pray for each other's families that week. I walked out lighter, like I had left a backpack of rocks under the table.

Reconciliation is not a shortcut. It is a road that starts with humility and keeps going with patience. Some doors will stay shut. As far as it depends on me, I want to knock with honest hands. That is worship in real time. It is how the kingdom breaks into ordinary life.

Prayer

Jesus, make me a peacemaker. Bring to mind the person I need to face. Give me courage to confess, listen, and repair. Strip away pride. Soften the other heart too. Guide my words toward truth and mercy. Let reconciliation become my worship today. Walk with me. Amen. Step by step.

A Moment with God

Who comes to mind when you pray about peace, and what is your first humble step toward them?

Practical Step

Write and send one genuine apology or start the process.

Week 23 - Hospitality without Performance

"Share with the Lord's people who are in need. Practice hospitality." (Romans 12:13)
Insight: Open homes open hearts.

I used to think guests required a magazine-ready table. I cleaned until I was cranky, then pretended to be cheerful when the doorbell rang. It felt fake. Romans 12 whispered a better path. Hospitality is not a show. It is a share. People need warmth more than perfect napkin folds.

So we tried something small. Soup and bread, Wednesday night. We texted two neighbors and an older widow from church. No fancy. Just a pot, a loaf, and a candle on the table. Our dog greeted everyone like they were heroes. We laughed about burnt toast stories. The widow told us about her husband's goofy whistle. My neighbor asked for prayer over job stress. We circled up in the kitchen, hands still damp from washing bowls, and asked Jesus for help. He came.

I did not apologize for dust. I did not hide our life. I offered it. When they left, the house looked a little messier and felt a lot holier. Hospitality without performance freed my heart to focus on people, not props.

The next morning, I wrote "Soup Night" on the calendar again. Open homes open hearts, including mine. I want our door to tell the truth about God's welcome. He meets us with bread enough for today and mercy for the crumbs we drop.

Prayer

God, open my door and my heart. Free me from performance and fear. Give me eyes to see needs, a table to share, and words that welcome. Make our home a simple refuge where strangers become friends and friends find rest. Use our meals for grace. Amen. Often and gladly.

A Moment with God

What simple meal and two guests could you invite this week so love takes the front seat?

Practical Step

Host a simple soup-and-bread night this week.

Week 24 - Gifts You Still Carry

"As each has received a gift, use it to serve one another, as good stewards of God's varied grace." (1 Peter 4:10)

The week after I turned in my work badge, I cleaned the garage like a man burying a chapter. My toolbox felt heavier than usual. The tape measure snapped back like it was annoyed at me. I held my old hard hat and wondered if the world still needed what I knew. Retirement had cleared my calendar, but it also cleared my confidence. I was good at fixing systems, training people, and troubleshooting problems. But who would ask now?

That Sunday the church projector died ten minutes before service. I stood in the back, pretending not to notice, until the verse came to mind about being a steward of God's grace. Steward is not a title you retire from. I slipped behind the sound booth, checked a cable, reset the input, and the screen sprang to life. No applause, just a few grateful nods. Later that afternoon, my neighbor's mailbox leaned like a tired soldier. I set it straight, tamped the dirt, and brushed my hands. He stepped out and said, "I kept putting that off. Thanks."

That evening I opened a notebook and wrote three headings: Training, Fixing, Encouraging. Under each, I listed specific ways those gifts could meet needs close by. I was surprised how quickly ideas landed on the page. A teen at church needed help with a resume. The community center's computers ran slow. A new dad down the street looked exhausted and could use a listening ear. The insight landed gently. My skills did not retire. The paychecks stopped, the stewardship continued. Gifts are not ornaments. They are tools in God's hands, placed in mine for the people right in front of me.

Prayer

Lord, You shaped me for service, not storage. Renew my joy in using what You gave. Open my eyes to real needs nearby, and give me courage to step in. Show me where my gifts meet needs, and make me a faithful steward of Your varied grace each day. Amen.

A Moment with God

Which gift have you quietly boxed up that God might want back in circulation this month?

Practical Step

List your top 3 skills. Match each to one local need you can serve in the next two weeks.

Week 25 - Your Service Lane

"We are his workmanship, created in Christ Jesus for good works, which God prepared beforehand, that we should walk in them." (Ephesians 2:10)

In my first months of retirement I said yes to everything. I stacked chairs at church, joined a food drive, signed up to read at a school, tried the hospital volunteer desk, and even considered coaching soccer. My calendar looked productive. My soul felt scattered. One afternoon my wife slid me a cup of coffee and said, kindly, "You are always busy, but you do not look alive." She was right. I was dabbling in ten things and deep in none.

During a sermon I had heard the phrase "prepared works." It kept echoing. Prepared means specific, not random. I prayed, then looked at my wiring. I like steady rhythms, mentoring, and practical problem solving. I scheduled three coffee meetings with leaders I respected and asked where a faithful, weekly presence could help. Each conversation pointed to the same place, a reading program at the elementary school. It was not flashy. It was focused.

The first day I sat with a second grader named Malik whose eyes danced but whose confidence stumbled over words. We sounded out syllables, celebrated small wins, and high-fived the last page. Walking home, I felt a clear sense of God's smile. I had entered a lane that fit how He made me. Focus beats dabbling. Peace replaced the pressure to say yes to everything. Ephesians 2:10 moved from a verse to my calendar. God prepared good works, and I could walk in them at a pace that honored Him and my family. The fruit did not come from doing more. It came from being faithful in the lane He assigned.

Prayer

Father, thank You for crafting good works ahead of me. Quiet my urge to chase everything. Give me clarity, courage, and a steady pace to walk in what You prepared. Guide me to prepared works and keep me faithful when serving feels small or slow today and each day. Amen.

A Moment with God

What one serving lane best fits your wiring, season, and weekly rhythm right now?

Practical Step

Pick one consistent serve lane for the next three months. Choose church, school, clinic, or shelter, and commit.

Week 26 - Mentor One Man

"What you have heard from me in the presence of many witnesses entrust to faithful men who will be able to teach others also." (2 Timothy 2:2)

At a men's breakfast, I noticed a younger guy hanging back after the crowd thinned. He kept tugging at his sleeve like his thoughts itched. I asked how he was doing. He shrugged, then said, "I am overwhelmed. New baby. New job. I want to lead my home well, but I do not know where to start." I nodded. I remembered that feeling like it was yesterday. Multiplication, not addition, came to mind. I did not need to attend five more events. I needed to pour into one man.

We met at a quiet diner every other Tuesday. We read a chapter of the Gospel of Mark out loud, swapped stories of what God was teaching us, and ended by praying for specific decisions. I shared a failure for each success so he knew I was not a superhero, just a man being shaped by grace. We talked money, marriage, work, and temptation. I gave him two simple assignments each time, then asked him to share what he learned with another younger guy. By week four, he was already encouraging a co-worker who was struggling.

The power of 2 Timothy 2:2 is simple. Truth entrusted keeps traveling when you hand it to someone who will hand it to someone else. I had spent years building reports and teams. Now I was building a man. The joy surprised me. It was slower than a program, but deeper. My calendar had fewer meetings, and my life had more meaning. Addition is me doing more. Multiplication is me equipping someone who equips someone else. That is how legacies grow.

Prayer

Lord Jesus, You entrusted truth to Your followers and multiplied it through them. Train my heart to invest, not impress. Give me one man to love, teach, and encourage. Entrust truth through me, and make us both obedient and bold for the next generation's good today, for Your glory. Amen.

A Moment with God

Who is one younger man you can invite to meet regularly for prayer, Scripture, and honest conversation?

Practical Step

Ask one younger man to meet biweekly for three months. Keep it simple and consistent.

Week 27 - Work Redefined

"Whatever you do, work heartily, as for the Lord and not for men." (Colossians 3:23)
A few months into retirement I missed the rhythm of a workday, the hum of purpose. One morning a widow from our church, Mrs. Alvarez, mentioned her porch light flickered and her back steps wobbled. I used to manage projects with big budgets. This looked small. I almost passed it to someone else. Then Colossians 3:23 tugged at me. Whatever you do. Not just impressive things. All things.

I grabbed my tools and headed over. The light just needed a new socket and tighter wiring. The steps needed fresh screws and a level hand. Mrs. Alvarez made cinnamon tea and told me about her husband who used to fix everything. The job took two hours. No paycheck. No applause. But as I tightened the last screw, I felt a quiet joy I had not felt in a while. The Lord was watching, and that changed the whole scene. The workbench became an altar. The drill sounded like worship.

That week I set aside one day for pro-bono work using my trade. I asked around and found a single dad who needed a ceiling fan installed, a neighbor whose fence gate sagged, and a small nonprofit with a balky copier. None of it would land on a resume. All of it mattered to God. Colossians 3:23 does not shrink our work. It expands it. When the audience is Jesus, mundane tasks become meaningful. Retirement did not end my labor. It reset my motive. I get to give my best in unseen places because the One who sees is pleased.

Prayer

Father, reframe my hands and habits. Teach me to work heartily for You, not for applause. Make hidden tasks fragrant offerings. Be glorified in my unseen labor, and help me serve with excellence, patience, and joy, especially when no one notices but You. I gladly offer today to You. Amen.

A Moment with God

Which ordinary task this week can you treat as worship by slowing down, doing it well, and praying as you work?

Practical Step

Offer one pro-bono day this month using your trade for someone in need.

Week 28 - Small and Steady Impact

"Seek the welfare of the city where I have sent you, and pray to the Lord on its behalf, for in its welfare you will find your welfare." (Jeremiah 29:7)

I used to think impact required a platform. Then I started walking my block with a trash grabber and a prayer list. It began on a Saturday. Our neighborhood app was buzzing about litter and loud music. I felt annoyed, then convicted. Jeremiah 29:7 says to seek the city's welfare. Seek means go after it. So I joined the monthly cleanup, learned the names of the folks who always showed up, and brought extra bags.

Small and steady started changing me. I picked up bottles, waved at dog walkers, and asked the Lord to bring peace to this street. At the neighborhood board meeting I listened more than I spoke. I learned we lacked a crosswalk near the park where kids sprinted between parked cars. A retired teacher, a young mom, and I drafted a polite request to the city. Two months later, paint lines and signs appeared. Not a revival. Still a mercy.

One afternoon Mr. Richardson, our gruff neighbor, watched me pull weeds at the corner. He grunted, then surprised me by handing over a cold water and saying, "Thanks for caring." We talked for ten minutes about his bad knee and his grandkids. I told him I would pray for his next doctor visit. He nodded, softening. Peace, it turns out, often comes through presence, not speeches. I am learning to be that presence. The impact is not headline worthy. It is holy ordinary. Seek the city's peace in small ways, and do it steady. The Lord is at work on every block.

Prayer

God of peace, anchor me in my place. Give me eyes for small needs and steady hands for ordinary service. Teach me to seek my city's welfare with prayer, presence, and practical help. Make me a bringer of peace, starting on my block, this week today, for Christ's sake. Amen.

A Moment with God

Where can you show up consistently in your neighborhood to bring peace through presence, prayer, and practical help?

Practical Step

Join a monthly neighborhood cleanup or attend one local board meeting. Learn one issue and help.

Week 29 - Share Your Testimony

"He drew me up from the pit of destruction, out of the miry bog, and set my feet upon a rock... He put a new song in my mouth, a song of praise to our God." (Psalm 40:2–3)

I put off telling my story because it felt messy. Years ago I lived in quiet anger. Work owned me. My kids got my leftovers. My wife prayed for me while I buried myself in deadlines. The pit was not obvious, but it was real. One night I snapped at my son over a spilled drink. His face crumpled, and so did I. I sat in the garage and finally said, "Lord, I am not who I want to be." A friend invited me to a men's group, and the gospel landed fresh. Jesus did not just forgive me. He started rebuilding me.

When I retired, the Lord nudged me to write a three-minute testimony. I used a simple outline. Before Jesus, how He met me, what changed since. I wrote in plain words, not churchy language. I included one failure, one Scripture, and one clear explanation of how to respond to Him. Then I practiced out loud until it fit in three minutes without rushing.

I shared it first at our group, voice shaking a little. Then, strangely enough, with my barber when he asked how I was handling retirement. I watched him lean in. My story was not dramatic, but it was honest. Psalm 40 says God puts a new song in our mouths so others will see and trust Him. Your rescue story is a tool, not a trophy. Keep it handy. Say it with humility. Let God decide where it lands.

Prayer

Lord, thank You for lifting me from pits I could not escape. Give me words and timing. Help me write clearly, speak humbly, and point to Jesus. Put a new song in my mouth that others might trust You because of Your rescue. Use my story for Your glory. Amen.

A Moment with God

If you had three minutes to tell your rescue story today, what would you say in thirty seconds for each part: before, how Jesus met you, after?

Practical Step

Write a three-minute testimony. Share it once this month with a friend, group, or neighbor.

Week 30 - Mission at Home Base

"You will receive power when the Holy Spirit has come upon you, and you will be my witnesses in Jerusalem and in all Judea and Samaria, and to the end of the earth." (Acts 1:8)

I used to dream about serving far away. Then I realized Jesus starts with Jerusalem, the place you already live. My "Jerusalem" has a cracked sidewalk, two maple trees, and a row of mailboxes where conversations begin. I decided to learn the names on my street and one prayer need for each. It felt simple. It felt scary too.

I started with the man two doors down who always wore a Titans cap. I said, "I am trying to be a better neighbor. I am Jim. What is your name?" He laughed and said, "Dan. Nice to finally meet you, Jim." We talked about his job, his mom's health, and the squeaky hinge on his gate. I asked if I could pray for his mom that week. He nodded. The next time I saw him, I asked how she was doing. He told me she was feeling better and that the hinge sounded happier too.

These tiny steps changed my posture. The Spirit's power shows up at mailboxes and fences just as surely as on mission trips. I started hosting a simple porch night once a month. I grilled hotdogs, asked about people's weeks, and listened more than I talked. When someone shared a burden, I offered to pray right there, short and sincere. Acts 1:8 is not only about distance. It is about direction. Start here, then see where God sends you.

Mission is not somewhere else someday. It is home, today, empowered by the Spirit who loves your block more than you do.

Prayer

Holy Spirit, empower my everyday witness. Make my home base a light. Help me learn names, needs, and stories, and respond with prayer and kindness. Give me courage at the mailbox, the fence, the store, and the table. Start in me, start here, start now today and every day. Amen.

A Moment with God

Who is one neighbor whose name and story you can learn this week, and what is one way you can serve or pray for them?

Practical Step

Learn one neighbor's name and one prayer need. Write it down and follow up within a week.

Week 31 - Body as Trust

"Do you not know that your bodies are temples of the Holy Spirit, who is in you, whom you have received from God? You are not your own. You were bought at a price. Therefore honor God with your bodies." — 1 Corinthians 6:19–20

My doctor did not say anything dramatic. He just slid his glasses down and tapped the chart. "Numbers are creeping up. Nothing scary, but they are talking to you." I laughed it off in the office, but the truth followed me home. That evening, my grandson handed me a foam football and shouted, "Race you to the tree!" I made it to the mailbox and felt my chest thump like a drum. He jogged back, cheeks flushed, still hopeful. I waved him on and said I needed a minute. He hid his disappointment, but I saw it anyway.

I used to treat my body like a pickup truck. As long as it started, I pushed it hard. Oil changes were optional. Retirement brought more sitting, more snacks, and fewer reasons to move. But that verse would not let me shrug. A temple is not mine to neglect. A temple is tended. Swept. Protected.

The next morning I laced up old walking shoes. The first ten minutes felt stiff. My knees complained. Then the air opened, and my breathing settled into a simple rhythm. I began to pray with each step. "Thank You." Step. "Help me." Step. "Use me." Step. By the end, I was not chasing a younger version of myself. I was returning a trust to its Owner.

I realized stewardship includes my body. Not to impress anyone, not to chase vanity, but to honor God with health that lets me love longer, serve steadier, and play catch without quitting at the mailbox.

Prayer

Lord, You paid a price for me. My body is Yours. Teach me to honor You in simple, steady choices. Give me courage to start small, to be consistent, and to see health as worship. Let strength serve love, and let my habits preach gratitude. Amen.

A Moment with God

Where is my body asking for care, and how will I answer God with one faithful change today?

Practical Step

Walk 20 minutes daily this week.

Week 32 - Strength in Weakness

"But he said to me, 'My grace is sufficient for you, for my power is made perfect in weakness.' Therefore I will boast all the more gladly about my weaknesses, so that Christ's power may rest on me." — 2 Corinthians 12:9

The fence post leaned like a tired soldier. I grabbed my tools and told my wife, "I have it." Halfway through digging, my shoulder sent a sharp warning. I paused, pretending to check my phone. Pride whispered, "Just push through." Pain answered, "Not today." I considered quitting quietly and telling no one. Then my neighbor, a young dad from down the street, called over the hedge, "Need a hand?"

Everything in me wanted to say no. I used to be the one who loaned ladders and lifted heavy things. But I nodded, and he came with a post hole digger and a simple grin. We worked together, taking slow turns. He asked about retirement, about marriage, about raising a son who will not nap. I told him I still wrestle with purpose. He said he wrestles with patience.

When the post finally stood straight, I put a hand on it and laughed. "Stronger than I am," I said. He looked at my shoulder. "I get it," he replied. We stood in the shade and I asked if I could pray for him. He said yes. We talked to God about a toddler who fights sleep and a man who fights pride. It was not a sermon. It was shared weakness in God's strong hands.

I always thought ministry flowed from my strength. That day it flowed from a limitation that made room for another person. Limits can become ministry when they open space for grace, honesty, and partnership. My weakness was not the end of usefulness. It was the door.

Prayer

Jesus, be strong in my weakness. Break my pride gently, and make room for Your power. Help me ask for help without shame, and offer help without superiority. Use my limits to build bridges, bless neighbors, and point to You, not me. Teach me to boast in grace. Amen.

A Moment with God

Where am I hiding a weakness that could become a doorway for connection and ministry if I brought someone in?

Practical Step

Ask for help in one task you usually hide.

Week 33 - Food as Provision

"Give us today our daily bread." — Matthew 6:11

For years I treated food like an enemy. Mondays began with strict rules. Fridays ended in a truce that tasted like cookies. I kept a running tally in my head that sounded like guilt. At a family dinner, my granddaughter brought out a loaf she had baked. The crust crackled. The kitchen filled with warm, buttery air. She beamed, waiting for my verdict. I felt the old war start. How many calories. How much will this set me back.

Then this simple prayer rose up from childhood: "Give us today our daily bread." Not tomorrow's. Not a punishment. Provision. I asked if we could bless the meal. We thanked God for the hands that kneaded the dough, for a table that gathers stories, for strength that comes from simple food. I took a slice. I ate slowly. I noticed my body relax as I received, instead of obsessing.

That week I opened my pantry and saw God's kindness stacked on shelves. Beans. Rice. Oats. Eggs in the fridge. It looked ordinary. It was holy. I stopped policing myself with shame and started planning like a steward. What meals would help me serve, move, and think clearly. What portions honored my needs and left room for joy.

Food is provision, not a battlefield. Gratitude turned down the volume of guilt. Planning turned down the volume of chaos. I still pass on seconds sometimes. I still enjoy dessert at birthdays. I have learned to bless the bread, not fear it, and to eat as a person loved by God, not judged by numbers alone.

Prayer

Father, thank You for today's bread. Teach me to receive food as Your care, not my enemy. Give me wisdom to choose what nourishes, and freedom from shame. Let my table be a place of peace, laughter, and gratitude. Feed my body and my soul. Amen.

A Moment with God

What one simple meal this week could I plan that would nourish me and remind me I am cared for by God?

Practical Step

Plan three simple, nourishing meals for the week.

Week 34 - A Quiet Mind

"Do not be anxious about anything, but in every situation, by prayer and petition, with thanksgiving, present your requests to God. And the peace of God, which transcends all understanding, will guard your hearts and your minds in Christ Jesus." — Philippians 4:6–7

It was 2 a.m. The ceiling fan hummed like a distant highway. My thoughts lapped the same anxious track. Savings. The roof. My adult kids' choices. The what ifs multiplied. I reached for my phone, then remembered a pastor's simple invitation. Train your mind to run toward God, not toward the worst case.

I sat up, feet on the carpet, and tried a breath prayer. Inhale, "Lord Jesus." Exhale, "I give this to You." I named the specific fears quietly. Roof. Health.

Family. Each time, I added thanksgiving. Thank You for a roof over my head tonight. Thank You for the doctor who listens. Thank You for children You love more than I do. My shoulders lowered. My jaw unclenched. It was not magic. It was practice.

The next day at lunch I set a timer for five minutes. I closed my eyes at the table, breathed slowly, and prayed the same way. I imagined handing Jesus a jumbled box of worries. He did not scold me. He placed a guarding hand over my heart and mind. Peace did not erase problems. It escorted me back into them with a steady step.

Prayer plus practice calms anxiety. I still get stirred up sometimes. But now I have a path, not just a verse on a mug. The path is simple. Present. Thank. Breathe. Repeat. Over time, peace becomes familiar, like a friend who sits beside you in the night and says, "I am here."

Prayer

Prince of Peace, guard my heart and mind in Christ. Train me to present my worries with thanksgiving. Meet me in the night and at noon. Let Your peace stand watch over my thoughts and guide my choices. Teach me to breathe grace in and fear out. Amen.

A Moment with God

Which three worries will I hand to Jesus today with specific thanksgiving attached to each?

Practical Step

5-minute breath-prayer at lunch daily.

Week 35 - Money with a Mission

"Command those who are rich in this present world not to be arrogant nor to put their hope in wealth, which is so uncertain, but to put their hope in God, who richly provides us with everything for our enjoyment. Command them to do good, to be rich in good deeds, and to be generous and willing to share." — 1 Timothy 6:17–19

I used to measure my life by totals at the bottom of statements. If the number was up, I felt secure. If it dipped, I felt shaky. One afternoon I met a man at church who had just started a new job through our benevolence ministry. He shook my hand with both of his. "Thank you for a bag of groceries two months ago," he said. "It kept me going."

I looked at my budget that night and saw a scoreboard where a mission should be. My money had been guarding my comfort instead of fueling my calling. The verse in Timothy gave me a new target. Hope in God, not returns. Be rich in good works, not just in accounts.

I printed three statements and a blank page. I asked two questions. What percent will we give. What purpose will we aim at. My wife and I prayed, then wrote a number that felt faithful and a list that felt focused. Local food stability. Young families in our church. A missionary friend we had forgotten to support consistently. We added one line called margin for surprise, so we could say yes when God nudged.

We did not give to feel superior. We gave to get in on what God already loves. Money is a tool, not a scorecard. In God's hands, it builds, feeds, and frees. In mine, it used to just sit and reassure. Now it moves.

Prayer

Provider, make me rich in good works. Shift my hope from wealth to You. Teach me to plan my giving with joy and purpose. Use my resources to meet real needs and point to real grace. Let generosity reorder my heart and bless others. Amen.

A Moment with God

If my money told a story, would it sound like comfort only, or like mission with purpose. What one change will I make?

Practical Step

Create a simple giving plan (percent + purpose).

Week 36 - Simplify to Bless

"Keep your lives free from the love of money and be content with what you have, because God has said, 'Never will I leave you, never will I forsake you.'" — Hebrews 13:5

The garage had become a museum of intentions. Extra tools, duplicate camping gear, boxes of cables for devices I no longer owned. I told myself I might need it all someday. The truth was, the clutter was costing me time, space, and peace. I bumped my shin on an old cooler and finally said out loud, "Enough."

I set up three piles. Keep. Give. Trash. The first ten minutes felt like pulling teeth. Then I found my father's old measuring tape. I kept it. Next, I found three hammers. I kept one. The other two went into the give pile. I pictured a young dad swinging one to build bunk beds. I pictured a widow's porch fixed by a volunteer with the other. My mood shifted. This was not losing. This was funding blessing.

By the end of the afternoon, the garage breathed again. So did I. My heart felt lighter, because contentment whispers, "You have enough." That verse reminded me the real anchor is God's presence, not more stuff. He will not leave me. Tools will. Trends will. He will not.

We loaded the car and donated useful items. The worker who received them smiled. "These will go fast." I drove home with space in the trunk and space in my soul. Contentment is not apathy. It is clarity. It frees resources, rooms, and hearts so generosity can move.

Prayer

Lord, teach me the gain of enough. Free me from fear that hoards. Show me what to keep and what to release. Let my simplicity become someone else's supply. Fill the empty spaces with Your presence and purpose, not more things. Make my home a channel of blessing. Amen.

A Moment with God

What clutter in my life is blocking generosity or peace, and what will I release this week with intention?

Practical Step

Declutter one room. Donate useful items.

Week 37 - Estate Wisdom

"A good person leaves an inheritance for their children's children." — Proverbs 13:22
When my father died, we found three versions of a will in different drawers, none signed. The week should have been for stories and hugs. Instead, it leaned toward confusion, phone calls, and strained voices. We all loved him. We just did not know his wishes. I told myself I would do better. Years passed. Papers piled up. The hard things stayed in a quiet stack.

One Saturday, I spread everything on the kitchen table. Insurance policies. Account statements. A half-filled beneficiary form. It felt heavy, like stepping into a storm. Then I thought of my children and their children. Wise planning is love in advance. This was not morbid. It was a gift.

I made a simple list. Will. Power of attorney. Healthcare directives. Beneficiaries. I wrote down where each item lived and what needed updating. I called an attorney and booked an appointment. I also wrote a letter for my family. Not about money. About faith, forgiveness, and the kind of legacy that outlives bank accounts. I told them I have made mistakes and met a faithful God. I told them what matters most and why.

By evening the stack was smaller, labeled, and clear. My heart matched it. Stewardship is not only about today's choices. It is also about tomorrow's burdens. When I plan, I lift weight from the shoulders I love. That is not fear. That is care.

Prayer

God of wisdom, give me foresight and fairness. Help me plan with calm hearts in mind. Show me how to protect, provide, and bless those I love. Let my legacy be more than wealth, shaped by faith and kindness. Guide every decision and conversation. Amen.

A Moment with God

If those I love had to find everything tomorrow, what would I wish I had prepared today, and what is my next faithful step?

Practical Step

List key documents (will, POA, beneficiaries) and book one appointment.

Week 38 - What Legacy Really Is

"One generation commends your works to another; they tell of your mighty acts." Psalm 145:4

My grandson and I were fishing at the old pond behind our church. The water was still, dragonflies skimming like tiny blue helicopters. He was quiet, watching the bobber, then asked, "Grandpa, what do you want people to remember about you?" I felt that question slide under my ribs. My first answer wanted to be a list: the career wins, the house we paid off, the trophies collecting dust. But the pond had a way of slowing me down to truth.

I thought about my dad, who did not leave me a lot of stuff. He left me a way of telling the truth even when it cost him. He left me the way he prayed before hard phone calls. He left me how he loved my mom when she was sick and scared. His legacy lived in how he walked with God, then handed that walk to me, one steady step at a time.

Legacy is not a grand speech or a statue in the park. It is truth plus love, handed over time. It is telling your family not only what God did, but how He did it in the dark, in the waiting, in the normal Tuesday. I told my grandson about the year I almost quit, the way Psalm 23 held me together, and how God sent three friends with casseroles and Scripture when my strength was thin. His eyes lit up more than when the first fish finally bit.

That day I realized the vineyard I am tending is not my name but God's works in my life, faithfully told. If I keep handing that over, little by little, the story will outlast me. The bobber dipped, he reeled in a small bass, and we both laughed. I think God smiled too.

Prayer

Lord, help me tell of Your works with honesty and warmth. Let my words be simple and strong, soaked in love and truth. Make my life a clear window where my family sees Your faithfulness, not my ego. Teach me what to pass on and how to pass it well. Amen.

Practical Step

Define your legacy in one paragraph. Write what you want your family to know about God from your life.

Week 39 - Ethical Will

"These commandments that I give you today are to be on your hearts. Impress them on your children... Write them on the doorframes of your houses." Deuteronomy 6:6-9

A box in my closet holds birthday cards, old photos, and a wrinkled program from my wedding. Tucked in that box is a letter from my grandmother. It is not fancy. No lawyer wrote it. She wrote about trusting Jesus when the crops failed, about telling the truth even when it cost money, about laughing often and forgiving faster. She called it her "heart letter." I did not know then, but that was an ethical will.

Stuff fades or breaks. Values outlast valuables. When I retired, I cleaned out my desk and realized nobody wanted my old awards. My granddaughter did want my stories of courage and my grandmother's recipe for mercy. Deuteronomy says truth belongs on our hearts and our doorframes. In other words, put it where you can see it, then pass it where others can live it.

I sat at the kitchen table and made a simple outline: beliefs, blessings, hopes. I wrote my core beliefs first: God is faithful when I am not. Jesus is enough when everything else is not. The Spirit guides when I ask. Then blessings: the people and moments where God showed up. Finally hopes: what I pray my family becomes when I am gone, not in careers but in character. I pictured their faces as I wrote, and my pen slowed at each name. It humbled me to realize I could sow seeds with sentences.

An ethical will is not a lecture. It is a lighthouse. It does not control the boat, it offers a steady beam. When the storms come, as they will, I want my family to see that light and remember the shoreline of God's truth.

Prayer

Father, write Your truth on my heart so I can write it on paper with love. Help my words bless, not boast. Make this ethical will a gentle guide, not a heavy rulebook. Let it point to You more than me and grow fruit after I am gone. Amen.

Practical Step

Draft a one-page ethical will. Include your core beliefs, blessings you see in your family, and hopes you pray over them.

Week 40 - Letters That Last

"The Lord bless you and keep you; the Lord make his face shine on you and be gracious to you..." Numbers 6:24-26

I found an old note in my toolbox, folded between a tape measure and a stubby pencil. It was from my wife, years ago: "Proud of how you kept your word. I see you." It was ten words, but it carried me through a hard week. Blessings do that. They multiply strength where fear tries to divide.

When my first grandson was born, I held him and felt the weight of time. I could not give him my years, but I could give him words he could carry into his years. Numbers 6 is a blessing that has traveled across centuries. It names what we need most: God's keeping, God's face, God's peace. Written down, it becomes a keepsake of grace.

So I pulled out paper and a pen, not the computer. Handwriting slows you enough to think. I thought about each child, each grandchild, their quirks and questions. I asked God for a word that matched their season. For one, courage. For another, patience. For another, joy that does not leak. I wrote how I see God at work in them, then spoke the blessing from Numbers 6 in my own voice: May the Lord steady your feet. May His smile warm your mornings. May His peace guard your nights.

Mail is rare now. That is why it matters more. When a real letter shows up, hearts open. Blessing by letter multiplies because it can be read again on hard days, shared at kitchen tables, tucked into Bibles. It reminds them not only that God is near, but that Grandpa is praying and cheering.

Prayer

God, put Your blessing in my words. Help me see each child the way You see them, then speak life with care and courage. Make my letters little altars where Your kindness meets their need. Use ink and paper to carry grace farther than my voice. Amen.

Practical Step

Handwrite a blessing letter to each child and grandchild. Name what you see God doing and speak Numbers 6 in your own words.

Week 41 - Story Vault

"Come and hear, all you who fear God; let me tell you what he has done for me." Psalm 66:16

My grandson loves my toolbox, but what he really wants is the story behind each scar on my hands. The Saturday he asked about the deepest scar, I almost waved it off. Then I saw the verse on a sticky note by the coffee maker: tell what God has done, specifically. Not vague. Not polished. Real.

So I told him about the night I sat in my truck outside the hospital, angry and afraid. I told him how I whispered a clumsy prayer, how a friend showed up with coffee at midnight, how the scan that scared us turned out different the next morning. I told him how I kept Psalm 27 in my pocket and read it like a map. His eyes got wide, not because Grandpa was brave, but because God met us in a parking lot.

A story vault is not about hoarding tales. It is about preserving faith fuel. When we forget specifics, we doubt faster. But when we remember the exact bend in the road where God carried us, faith stands taller. Recording stories is a way of stacking kindling for your family's fires later.

I pulled out my phone, hit record, and told three five-minute stories: the layoff that led to a better path, the apology that mended years of silence, the sunrise on a men's retreat when God felt closer than breath. I kept it plain. I named what I felt, what I prayed, what God did. I saved them in a folder called "Grandpa Stories." It felt small, but it was seed in the ground.

Prayer

Lord, make me a faithful witness. Give me courage to be specific, humble to share my weakness, and wisdom to point to Your strength. Use these stories to spark faith when doubt feels heavy. Let my simple words become reminders of Your mighty works. Amen.

Practical Step

Record three five-minute audio stories of God's faithfulness. Name the fear, the prayer, and what God did.

Week 42 - Photos With Purpose

"In the future, when your children ask you, 'What do these stones mean to you?'… these stones are to be a memorial." Joshua 4:6-7

We cleaned out the guest room closet and found boxes of random photos. Blurry sunsets. Ten pictures of the same birthday cake. A hundred shots without a story. My daughter laughed, then said, "Dad, which ones matter?" That question turned into a holy assignment.

When Joshua stacked stones from the Jordan, he did not make art, he made memory. Those stones were a sermon for the next generation. Our photos can be the same. Not every picture deserves a frame. The ones that mark God's faithfulness do.

I spread the photos on the kitchen table and asked two questions: Where did God meet us? What do I want them to remember? I picked the picture of the small apartment where we learned contentment. The snapshot of Mom in the chemo cap, grinning, surrounded by church friends. The baptism day at the lake. The bread we baked for neighbors during a storm. Each image got a short caption, simple and clear: "God provided when the budget was tight." "Joy in the fight." "Buried with Christ, raised to new life." "We serve because He served us first."

I watched my grandchildren lean over the table, pointing and asking. The photos became stones that preached. They drew out stories, prayers, and laughter. The album told them not just what we did, but what God did.

A camera can collect clutter, or it can curate a testimony. Choose the second. Let pictures become a path of praise your family can walk when you are not there to guide them.

Prayer

God, use our memories to magnify You. Help me choose photos that tell of Your goodness, not my pride. Give me simple words to frame each moment with truth. Make this album a doorway to stories that strengthen faith for years to come. Amen.

Practical Step

Curate a 20-photo "faith album" with short captions that name God's faithfulness in each moment.

Week 43 - Skill Transfer

"He has filled them with skill… and he has given both him and Oholiab the ability to teach others." Exodus 35:34-35

My workshop smells like cedar and coffee. Little hands love to wander in, pressing buttons they should not press. One Saturday, my grandson stood at the doorway, nervous. "Can I try?" I almost said, "Maybe when you are older." Then Exodus nudged me. Skill is a gift, and gifts are meant to be taught, not hoarded.

I pulled out a scrap board and started with safety, then showed him how to sand with the grain. His first try was rough. He frowned. I told him about my first crooked birdhouse and how my dad cared more about my character than my corners. "In this shop," I said, "we do not rush, we do not quit, and we clean up our mess." His shoulders relaxed. He smiled when the wood became smooth under his fingers.

Teaching a craft is teaching a way of being. Patience, integrity, attention, courage. When you let a child into your lane, you are not just passing a skill, you are shaping a soul. We built a simple shelf that day, slow and steady. I let him make small decisions. We prayed before we turned on the drill. We celebrated at the end, not because it was perfect, but because he grew.

I looked around at my tools and realized my real legacy was not the projects on the wall, it was the person standing beside me, hands dusty, heart awake. That shelf will hold books, but the lesson will hold him.

Prayer

Lord, help me train hands and hearts. Give me patience to teach slowly, grace to let them try, and courage to connect every skill to Your character. Use my shop, my garden, or my laptop to grow wisdom and work that honors You. Amen.

Practical Step

Plan a half-day "Grandpa Workshop" in your lane, whether wood, garden, cooking, mechanics, or coding. Teach the craft and the character behind it.

Week 44 - Family Summit Mini

"By wisdom a house is built, and through understanding it is established... its rooms are filled with rare and beautiful treasures." Proverbs 24:3-4

Most families drift into busyness without noticing. We pass like ships in the night, plates clinking, calendars overflowing. One month, small misunderstandings piled up in our house like laundry. I kept thinking, We need a table, not a text thread. Proverbs says wisdom builds a house and understanding fills it. That sounds like a gathered family.

So we tried a mini family summit. Nothing fancy. Just a 90-minute check-in around the table. We started with stories, each person sharing one win and one weight. It opened the room. Then we looked at the calendar, not to cram more in, but to guard space for what matters. Finally, we prayed for one another by name. The mood shifted from scattered to settled.

I saw my son soften when his sister shared something hard. I watched my granddaughter beam when we celebrated her science fair project. The room filled with treasures that do not break: listening, empathy, laughter, prayer. A shared table is where wisdom grows legs.

The summit does not fix everything. But it creates a rhythm where problems are named before they harden and gratitude is spoken before it fades. It turns a house back into a home.

Prayer

Father, build our house with understanding. Give us humble ears and gentle words. Help us make space to listen, plan, and pray together. Protect our unity, heal small fractures, and fill our rooms with the treasures of love, truth, and peace. Amen.

Practical Step

Host a 90-minute family check-in. Share stories, review the calendar, and pray for one another. Keep phones away and hearts open.

Week 45 - Legacy Of Generosity

"Whoever sows sparingly will also reap sparingly... God loves a cheerful giver... And God is able to bless you abundantly." 2 Corinthians 9:6-8

When I was a kid, my dad kept an envelope in the kitchen drawer marked "Seeds." It held cash for surprise needs. Groceries for a neighbor. Camp money for a kid. He never made a speech about generosity. He simply let me see him sow. Years later, I realized those small seeds turned into trees that still give shade.

Retirement can tempt us to hold tight. Budgets change, fears whisper. But the field of faith still waits for seed. Generosity is taught by doing, side by side. I told my family we were going to choose a cause together. We researched, prayed, and picked a local shelter that helped families get back on their feet. We gave as a team, then we visited.

We met a dad learning new skills, a mom smiling with a fresh start, kids playing in a safe room. My grandchildren asked a lot of questions. We served lunch, cleaned a play area, and listened. On the ride home, the car felt lighter. We had given money and time, but what changed most was our hearts. The verse came alive. God's abundance does not flow to closed fists. It flows to open hands.

I set a new envelope in our drawer and wrote "Seeds" on it. We agreed to keep sowing together, trusting God to grow what we cannot.

Prayer

Generous God, make us cheerful givers. Free us from fear and stinginess. Show us where to sow, and let us see faces, not just numbers. Use our giving to meet needs and to shape our hearts to look more like Yours. Fill our home with Your abundant grace. Amen.

Practical Step

Choose a cause together. Give as a family, then schedule a visit to serve or learn. Let the experience shape your future giving.

Week 46 - Endure the Long Mile

Let us run with patience the race set before us, looking to Jesus the author and finisher of our faith. (Hebrews 12:1-2)

The park opens early, and so do my knees. I used to sprint through mornings with a briefcase and a calendar. Now I jog the cracked lane around the baseball field, passing a bent fence and a drinking fountain that always drips. My grandson asked me to do a charity 5K with him. I said yes before my ankle could vote.

The first lap felt easy. The second reminded me I have a birthday coming. By the third, I started bargaining. Maybe I could "power walk" and call it good. Then I noticed an older man in a bright yellow cap, steady as a clock, never fast, never stopping. He nodded each time we met. He was not racing anyone. He was faithful to his pace.

That verse came to mind, the one about running with patience and fixing our eyes on Jesus. Finishing well is not a single victory lap. It is a daily choice. Not just with running, but with life. Do I grab the donut or the apple? Scroll late or sleep early? Complain about aches or thank God for breath? Hold a grudge or lay it aside? The "weights" are not always heavy. Sometimes they are soft and sticky, like comfort that slowly traps you.

Halfway through lap four, I named one weight: late-night mindless scrolling.

It steals my sleep and my morning focus. So I decided to put the phone in a drawer after dinner and pick up my Bible or call a friend. The yellow cap man finished his laps and waved. I kept going, slower, eyes up, heart steady.

Endurance grew inside me by inches, not leaps. The finish line mattered less than the One I was looking at. That is how I want to end my life too. Not with a sprint that burns out, but with steady steps, each day choosing to keep my eyes on Jesus.

Prayer

Jesus, set my focus on You. When I feel tired or distracted, steady my heart. Show me the weight I must lay aside today and give me courage to act. Grow patient endurance in me, one step at a time, until I finish well for Your glory and lasting joy.

A Moment with God

What one "weight" is slowing your race with Jesus, and what simple swap will you make tonight to lay it aside?

Practical Step

Identify one weight to lay aside; act today.

Week 47 - Walking Through Loss

The Lord is near to those who are of a broken heart; and saves those of a contrite spirit. (Psalm 34:18)

The chair stayed empty for weeks after my friend Harold passed. Same dent in the cushion. Same coffee ring on the coaster he never used right. I kept catching myself talking toward that chair during football, like he might answer with a groan about our team's defense. Grief sneaks up like that. It visits you at the mailbox, in the cereal aisle, in the quiet before bed.

I thought I had to be tough. Men do not cry, at least that is what I learned from my dad. But the night I found Harold's old text thread, I cried hard, shoulders shaking in the dark. I felt foolish until Psalm 34 lit up in my mind: God is near to the brokenhearted. Not annoyed. Not distant. Near.

The next morning, I took a slow walk and talked to God out loud. I told Him I hated death. I told Him I missed dumb jokes and shared silence. I told Him I was angry that the world kept moving like nothing happened. Then I said, "If this is a valley, help me walk it, not camp in it."

Later that week I met Sam from our men's group for coffee. I named the loss, not just Harold, but the piece of myself that laughed easier when he was around. Sam nodded. We prayed there at the sticky table. I did not feel fixed. I felt held.

Grief is a valley, not my address. I am passing through, and I am not alone. God's nearness does not erase the ache, but it steadies my steps. Some days are two steps forward, one step back. That is still movement. The empty chair still hurts, but now it points me toward a fuller table coming, where every tear will be wiped away.

Prayer

Father, be near to my broken heart. Hold the parts I cannot fix. Teach me to mourn with hope, to take the next step, and to receive Your comfort. Bring a brother to stand with me, and give us words and silence that heal. You are close to me today.

A Moment with God

What loss do you need to name before God and a brother, and what is the next small step through this valley?

Practical Step

Name one loss; share it with a brother; pray together.

Week 48 - Forgive Debts and Debtors

Forgive us our debts, as we forgive our debtors. (Matthew 6:12)

Years ago, I helped a business partner get through a rough season. I floated him cash and trust. The deal went bad, and so did our friendship. He never paid me back, and I kept him on a running tab in my head. Every time his name came up, my jaw got tight. I told myself I was being wise. Truth was, I was getting old from the inside out.

Unforgiveness ages the soul. It creases you in places no cream can reach. I noticed it in my tone with my wife and the way I replayed arguments while brushing my teeth. It was not just about money. It was about insisting that I be the judge and the jailer.

One morning, while praying through the Lord's Prayer, I could not slide past "forgive us our debts." I wanted God's grace like clean water. Then the next line hit like a mirror. If I wanted to live under mercy, I had to give it away. Forgiveness is not pretending it did not hurt. It is handing the gavel to Jesus and walking out of the courtroom free.

So I wrote a letter. I named the wrong, the cost, and my choice to forgive. I told him I was releasing him to God's care and justice and asking God to bless his family. I did not send it that day. I read it to the Lord. Peace came like a slow exhale. The knot in my chest softened. Later, I decided to mail it as an act of obedience, not outcome. He never replied. But I sleep better. My laugh came back.

Forgiveness does not erase memory. It drains the poison. It restores my hands for work and my heart for worship. As I have been forgiven, so I forgive.

Prayer

Lord, as I have been forgiven, help me forgive. Take the knot in my chest and soften my memory with mercy. Guard my words, release my hands from revenge, and let me bless those who hurt me. Make me free, whole, and useful for Your purposes today by Your grace.

A Moment with God

Who sits on the "debtor list" in your heart, and what would a simple obedience step toward forgiveness look like today?

Practical Step

Write one forgiveness letter (send or keep as obedience).

Week 49 - Courage to Witness

Be ready always to give an answer to every man that asks you a reason of the hope that is in you with meekness and fear. (1 Peter 3:15)

I met Joe at the hardware store. He is the guy who knows which screw you actually need, even when you do not. We swap fishing stories and small talk. I have prayed for him for months, waiting for a neon sign that says, "Share now." It never flashed. I kept quiet, telling myself I was just building trust.

Then last Tuesday, Joe said, "You seem… steady. What's your secret?" My heart thumped. I almost changed the subject to boat motors. Instead, I remembered 1 Peter 3: be ready. Hope speaks when asked and when nudged.

I have learned to keep a three-minute testimony in my pocket. Simple. No drama needed. Before Jesus, I chased approval and worried every night. I met Him when a friend invited me to church during a hard season. I heard that God loved me, not for what I did, but for what Jesus did. I trusted Him.

61

Since then, I still face problems, but I have peace in the storm and a purpose bigger than myself.

So I told Joe that. I did not preach. I asked about his story. He shared about a divorce and a daughter he is trying to reconnect with. We stood by the paint samples and prayed softly. No angels sang. But something holy happened between two men in aisle six.

Courage is not noise. It is love with a voice. Gentleness does not mean silence. It means respect. I still carry my little testimony, and I ask God for open doors and open ears. The pressure is not on me to convince. My part is to be clear, kind, and ready.

Prayer

Jesus, make me ready to answer with hope and to speak when You nudge. Give me courage with gentleness, clarity with kindness, and love that listens. Fill my mouth with simple truth about what You have done for me. Use my story for Your glory today in every open moment.

A Moment with God

If someone asked you today why you have hope, what are the three simple beats of your story you would share?

Practical Step

Share your 3-minute testimony with one person.

Week 50 - Joy in the Ordinary

Whether you eat, or drink, or whatever you do, do all to the glory of God. (1 Corinthians 10:31)

Saturday looked plain. The sink was full. The grass was long. The mailbox creaked. A younger me would have rushed through chores like a race to get to the "real" stuff. Retirement taught me something surprising. The "real" stuff lives inside the chores.

I started with dishes. Warm water. Bubbles popping. I prayed for each person whose cup I rinsed. I fixed the squeaky hinge on the pantry and asked God to make me a quiet hinge in my home. I mailed a handwritten note to a neighbor who lost his job, slipped a grocery gift card inside, and said nothing to anyone. No camera. No post. Just a hidden kindness between me and the Lord.

At lunch, I cut an apple and thanked God for the crisp snap and the juice that ran down my thumb. Later, I mowed straight lines and talked to God about my kids. I felt silly at first. Then the yard looked neat and so did my heart. Joy rose not from fireworks, but from faithfulness.

God is glorified in small faithfulness. When He fills the ordinary, it becomes holy ground. Folding a towel can be worship. A short text can be a lifeline. A quiet "thank You" while changing a lightbulb can shape a soul. It shaped mine.

By evening, the house felt lighter. My wife smiled at the pantry door that no longer groaned. We ate simple soup and laughed about an old story. I went to bed tired in the best way, like I had spent the day inside a prayer.

Prayer

Father, sanctify my ordinary. Teach me to sweep floors, write emails, and wash dishes with a worshiping heart. Meet me in hidden places where only You see. Use small faithfulness to shape me like Christ and to bless others without applause. Let joy rise in simple things today and tomorrow.

A Moment with God

What common task will you do today as a quiet act of worship, and how will you remind yourself to do it with God?

Practical Step

Do one hidden good deed today.

Week 51 - Anticipate Heaven

For to me to live is Christ, and to die is gain. (Philippians 1:21)

After the funeral, I sat on the porch with a worn Bible and a heavy chest. Clouds moved slow like freight trains. I turned to Revelation 21 and read about a new heaven and a new earth, a city where God wipes away every tear, where death does not exist. The words felt too good for a day that hurt. But hope is not a bandage. It is fuel.

I remembered my friend's worn hands and the way he greeted everyone by name. He is not less alive now. He is more. That changed how I felt about my own calendar. If living is Christ and dying is gain, then today matters more, not less. Heaven does not make earth small. It makes it meaningful.

I set a timer for five minutes and pictured the promises. No pain behind my knees. No goodbyes at hospital doors. Faces lit by the presence of Jesus. A table long enough for every story and every healed scar. The ache inside me loosened, not because I escaped life, but because I saw it straight. The finish line is real. Joy is not wishful thinking. It is my future address.

I called my grandson and asked about his science project. I checked on a neighbor who lost his wife last winter. I prayed for our pastor. The hope of heaven did not pull me away. It pushed me in.

When fear about death whispers at night, I answer with Scripture and the memory of that porch. My Savior beat death. My citizenship is secure. Until then, I want to live like a man who knows where home is and who is coming soon.

Prayer

Lord, set my hope fully on You. Let heaven's promises clean my eyes so I can see today clearly. Heal my fears about death, renew my courage to live, and make me eager for Your presence. Let this hope fuel love and steady service in my home and community today.

A Moment with God

Which promise from Revelation 21 most strengthens you, and how will you let that hope shape one choice you make today?

Practical Step

Meditate 5 minutes on heaven's promises (Revelation 21).

Week 52 - Your Rule of Life

A man's heart plans his way, but the Lord directs his steps. (Proverbs 16:9)

I spread a clean sheet of paper on the kitchen table and poured coffee like I was clocking in for something important. I wrote five words across the top: faith, family, service, stewardship, rest. Not fancy. Just lanes for the road ahead. Retirement freed my schedule. It also exposed how easy it is to drift.

A rule of life is not a prison. It is a trellis that helps your life grow in the right direction. I thought about faith first. I circled "Scripture before screens" and "Sabbath dinner candle." For family, I wrote "date night Thursdays" and "call each grandchild monthly." Service became "check on two neighbors weekly" and "mentor one younger man." Stewardship looked like "give first" and "track spending on Sundays." Rest included "walks without earbuds" and "one hobby for joy."

I prayed over each line, asking God to direct steps, not just bless plans. Some ideas felt too heavy. I crossed them out. This was not about building a new law. It was about choosing direction over drift. I penciled checkboxes for rhythms and left room for grace, because life is not a straight line.

By lunch, I held a one-page rule, simple enough to fit in my Bible. I showed my wife and asked for her wisdom. She smiled and added one request: "Leave margin for surprises." Good call. God often shows up in the margins.

The next morning, I started with Scripture before screens and lit that small candle. The room felt different. So did I. A paper will not change my life. Obedience will. But the paper made obedience simpler to choose each day.

Direction beats drift. The Lord will adjust my route as needed. My job is to start, step, and stay teachable.

Prayer

Father, establish my plans in Your will. Order my days, correct my steps, and close paths that do not honor You. Give me a simple rule that protects what matters most. Help me keep it with grace, courage, and joy as You guide my year for Your name's great glory.

A Moment with God

Looking at faith, family, service, stewardship, and rest, where is God nudging you to set one simple rhythm this week?

Practical Step

Finalize a one-page rule of life for the next year (faith, family, service, stewardship, rest).

www.ingramcontent.com/pod-product-compliance
Lightning Source LLC
Chambersburg PA
CBHW020421150626
46554CB00014B/2341